ELEGIES

To Carla,
Thanks for your gracious hospitality and your great tip about Ice House — it was one of the highlights of the trip.

With appreciation

Janet Jsmith
(1-24-2010)

THE TRIBUTE OF HIS PEERS

ELEGIES

FOR ROBINSON JEFFERS

EDITED

WITH AN INTRODUCTION BY

ROBERT ZALLER

TOR HOUSE PRESS

© 1989 Tor House Press

ISBN 0-9622774-0-1

*This volume has been made possible through
the generous assistance of Carol Onofrio,
in memory of her husband, Lou Onofrio,
who treasured the poetry of Robinson Jeffers,
was sustained by it in battle for his country,
and lived with it all his life.*

CONTENTS

INTRODUCTION
ROBERT ZALLER

xv

★

THE POET IS DEAD
WILLIAM EVERSON

1

THE STONE-MASON
TIM REYNOLDS

11

THE RETURN OF ROBINSON JEFFERS
ROBERT HASS

15

TO ROBINSON JEFFERS
CZESLAW MILOSZ

21

FOR ROBINSON JEFFERS
ALAN WILLIAMSON

27

FAILED TRIBUTE TO THE STONEMASON OF TOR HOUSE

JAMES TATE

31

AFTER READING ROBINSON JEFFERS

WILLIAM STAFFORD

35

DEAR JEFFERS

WILLIAM PITT ROOT

39

THOUGHTS OF JEFFERS AND TOR HOUSE

TIM HUNT

43

JEFFERS' HOUSE

JOHN BRUGALETTA

47

YOM KIPPUR 1984

ADRIENNE RICH

53

CAP OF DARKNESS
DIANE WAKOSKI
63

HOMAGE TO ROBINSON JEFFERS
PETER DALE
69

FOR ROBINSON JEFFERS
WILLIAM HOTCHKISS
73

POET, BE WITH ME
ROBERT ZALLER
79

I have incurred a more than ordinary number of debts in preparing this volume. I would like to thank particularly the past and current presidents of the Robinson Jeffers Tor House Foundation, George L. White and Jean Ritter-Murray, for their encouragement, support, and assistance; Nancy Miller, the former Executive Director of the Foundation; James Karman; John Varady; and, on behalf of all those connected with the Foundation as well as myself, Carol Onofrio. I cannot properly thank but cannot omit to mention my wife, Lili, who stood by the gestation of this small, but, I think, important book of testimony very much like a Jeffers heroine herself.

Robert Zaller
20 September 1988

INTRODUCTION

It was Horace Gregory who called Robinson Jeffers "a poet without critics" in the 1950s, when his reputation was at low ebb. This is no longer the case. Since the appearance of Radcliffe Squires' *The Loyalties of Robinson Jeffers* in 1956, there has been a steady stream of Jeffers scholarship, with monographic studies appearing every three or four years on average, and a score of significant theses and dissertations. Nonetheless, the critical yield on Jeffers is still far short of what a poet of his stature might expect.

The relative default of the critics, however, has proved the opportunity of the poets. Jeffers is one of the few poets of his generation who can still be discovered afresh, without the weight of critical exegesis that burdens an Eliot or a Pound. In their search for a usable past, therefore, a tradition unencumbered by the judgments of the academy, the poets of the present generation have turned to Jeffers and established their own dialogue with him. Their tributes testify in the most eloquent way to Jeffers' continuing relevance, for it is not the critics who constitute the tradition but the poets themselves, who pass along the living word from generation to generation. By this measure, indeed, Jeffers may be as "influential" in contemporary verse as any poet of this century.

The pattern of these tributes was set by

William Everson's great elegy, "The Poet Is Dead," which was written for and read at a celebration in Jeffers' honor shortly after his death in 1962. In Everson's poem, Jeffers is never mentioned by name; he is simply and archetypally "the poet." The effect is emphasized by the use of the definite article to describe his personal attributes:

The great tongue is dried.
The teeth that bit to the bitterness
Are sheathed in truth.

The clinical effects of death—the chilled seed, the pinched toes—are set side by side with passages that describe ongoing natural life:

If you listen
You can hear the field mice
Kick little spurts in the grasses. . .
Over the salt marsh the killdeer,
Unrestrainable,
Cry fear against moonset.

The processes of nature are "unrestrainable," whether the ordinary persistence of life or the onset of decay. Nature and the poet are thus unified, and by metaphor made interchangeable:

The caged ribs and the bladed shoulders,
Ancient slopes of containment,
Imperceptibly define the shelves of structure,

Faced like rock ridges
Boned out of mountains, absently revealed
With the going of the snow.

Much of the force of Everson's poem comes from his refusal to choose between the grieving recognition of death ("For the poet is dead... I tell you/ The nostrils are narrowed. I say again and again/ The strong tongue is broken") and the implied identity of the poet and nature in death. A similar tension is maintained between the indifferent processes of decay and the "old mother" who "grieves her deathling" and hunts him in the dark. Both perspectives are valid, the singularity of the poet's death and its perfect naturalness, the persistence of organic process and the indefinable grief that tragedy, as Jeffers himself suggested, permits us to impute to its workings. That is to say, the poem is self-consciously Jeffersian itself, though Jeffers would hardly have permitted such importance to be attached to individual human life. There are deliberate references to Jeffers' own verse, for example in the allusions to the "treacherous woman called Life... Blond and a harlot," and "The gaunt wolf" who "Crawled out to the edge and died snapping."[1] This is tribute

---

1. Cf. "To Death" and "The Deer Lay Down Their Bones," in *Hungerfield and Other Poems* (New York: Random House, 1954).

rather than imitation, of course, since Everson is far too strong a poet to need borrowed images. The essence of his praise is to evoke the Jeffersian cosmos—the world Jeffers uniquely created—and to lay him finally to rest in it.

Tim Reynolds' "The Stone-Mason" is dated 1958 but was not published in book form until after Jeffers' death,[2] and its elegiac tone qualifies it for inclusion among the rest. Like Everson, Reynolds evokes the Jeffers landscape, and even the long Jeffers line; but with a difference:

*I have watched hawks in updraft effortlessly
    lifting,*
*wings wide: seen redwoods' strength and
    cypresses' warped endurance;*
*sea-carved granite headlands plumbing sheer
    down, bicep-curved, to sea;*
*half-seen deer—seen, but never freshly, all this
    having been claimed by*
*him who staked out this land, these
    permanences, unalienably for his.*

Reynolds' disclaimer is too modest, for the "bicep-curved" headlands is surely a fine image in its own right. But the sense of redundancy, of having arrived late in a land whose "permanences" are the property of another, echoes in its way Ever-

---

[2]. In *Ryoanji: Poems* (New York: Harcourt, Brace, and World, 1964).

son's identification of Jeffers with the coastal landscape and the timelessness of its processes. Another theme is joined here too which will figure prominently in later elegies, the contemporary poet's sense of personal inadequacy before the monumental and somehow inaccessible figure of Jeffers:

And I have seen him, who quarried out and
    worked this raw existence,
the stone-mason: seen him walking by day in
    the shade of the big trees
framing the tower of boulders he hung against
    the sky . . .

Reynolds has "seen" the poet but not approached him, as if, like one of the apparitions Jeffers himself describes, he were a fact of wonder rather than a literary colleague. Reynolds' dilemma, therefore, is not merely that of a latecomer who finds a particular piece of ground "staked out," but of a successor who confronts so daunting an achievement that his own powers are called into question: itself an ironic replication of Jeffers' own characteristic portrayals of weak sons overshadowed by imperious fathers. By recreating the Big Sur coast as "something more lucid than any visible light, lighter than fog/ lifting still higher than hawk-flight," yet still "tough as backbones of coastal hills," Jeffers has in some sense entered the landscape itself and become part of its permanence. Not, indeed, a man easy to converse with: and we have Everson's own testimony of his principled avoidance for thirty years of the man he acknowledged as his poetic master, yet never met.

In Reynolds' poem, Jeffers, though perhaps literally glimpsed by him while still alive, already appears as a kind of ghost, "lighter than fog" and yet, to use one of Jeffers' own figures, "laired in rock."[3] It is not surprising, then, to find Jeffers' ghost evoked in Robert Hass' "The Return of Robinson Jeffers." The Jeffers-persona of his poem finds himself back among the coastal hills, but he cannot "say what brought him back." Hass recalls what appears to be Jeffers' little-remembered poem "Resurrection," in which a dead lover comes back from the grave to claim his promised bride, though in Hass' version it is her desire that calls him back. The poem ends with the lovers going off to their impossible consummation, and Hass faults Jeffers for not writing the sequel, because "Human anguish made him cold." This, he suggests, is what has brought Jeffers back: matchless in his abil-

---

3. Cf. "Soliloquy," in Tim Hunt, ed., *The Collected Poetry of Robinson Jeffers*, Vol. I (Stanford: Stanford University Press, 1988), p. 215.

ity to evoke human passion, he refused finally to suffer it, and was therefore justly required (not unlike the Jesus of Jeffers' own "Dear Judas") to answer for his sin of pride and his own unpurged passion. He must feel "rage" and "desire," and find brotherhood with "the world's numb poor/ His poems had despised." Hass imagines Jeffers feeling the pain of love "like the first dark/ Stirrings of a child" in the womb, feminizing him in a calculated reversal of the masculine transformations of such Jeffers characters as Tamar or April Barclay. Only then, as a penitent, can he find fulfillment and final release.

Czeslaw Milosz's "To Robinson Jeffers" presents a similarly ambiguous and conflicted response to Jeffers. Milosz contrasts the homely, simple, affectionate world of his forefathers, "a childhood/ prolonged from age to age," with the violence of Jeffers' Scotch-Irish ancestors. There is no effort here to reconcile opposed values, however, nor to soften the perceived rigidity of Jeffers' vision. "If you have not read the Slavic poets," Milosz apostrophizes him, "so much the better." As Hass accuses Jeffers of giving himself to "stone gods," so Milosz describes him as "Thin-lipped, blue-eyed, without grace or hope,/ before God the Terrible, body of the world," and wonders, "What have I to do with you?" He tells Jeffers that despite his insistence on a truth without consolation—or perhaps because of it—"you did not know what I know," and concludes:

Better to carve suns and moons on the joints of
   crosses
as was done in my district. To birches and firs
give feminine names. To implore protection
against the mute and treacherous night
than to proclaim, as you did, an inhuman
   thing.

At the same time, however, Milosz is clearly challenged by this alien vision. It forces him to rethink his own comfortable world, more humanly scaled yet not without its own "futile creeds," and a willful naivete that inspires more nostalgia than respect in the mature poet. There is a grudging but very real admiration for this fellow poet encountered at the farthest verge of a new land, "so brave in a void." If Jeffers' vision cannot be accepted, must even be rejected, it cannot be dispelled. The tribute of negation is, in this case, perhaps even dearer than that of praise.[4]

Milosz maintains a tone of conversational address, but in Alan Williamson's

---

4. Cf. the more balanced appreciation in Milosz's essay, "Carmel," in *Visions from San Francisco Bay* (New York: Farrar, Straus, and Giroux, 1982), pp. 87–94.

"For Robinson Jeffers," what begins in a similar vein—"More and more I think about you"—ends in an effort not merely to evoke Jeffers' tone but to instate his voice. Williamson reflects on those who, like Jeffers (though he names no others), chose to "harden their difference," to seek an isolate integrity of witness. In an age of glib analysis, such attitudes are easily dismissed:

> *Oh, I know*
> *all one might say: that what you fled and resented*
> *was the father within; or, worse, some incapacity*
> *you half-knew in yourself, and could not cure;*
> *that the more your peace was accomplished, the harder a spectral*
> *humanity seethed from behind the planted forest,*
> *from the cities as you dreamed them . . . till the love of yourself you began with*
> *half-recoiled at the self it had made. . .*

Williamson's analysis, of course, is far from glib, and by the end of the stanza he has vividly caught the dilemma, so often pondered by Jeffers himself, of a self-abnegating narcissism. But, as Williamson suggests, it is only by such a descent into the self, however flawed the circumstances or partial the result, that new truth is won. Like Hass, he brings Jeffers back, not however as a penitent but to speak in his own defense. Those who have chosen to "elaborate the surface," his "Jeffers" says—not to praise the God-informed beauty of things but to reproduce the textures of illusion—become that surface itself, a "celluloid" barely distinguishable from what it describes. They forsake the very function of poetry, which is to define the human against the dark glory of the cosmos, leaving nothing "even to wish for." Without desire—the effort to appropriate the real, to contest it, to transcend it—there is no humanity, but only envy, incapacity, and hatred. Thus it is not for his faults that he is hated, Williamson's Jeffers avers, "*but because/ I wished to walk out of myself in a soul and a body.*"

A similar blurring between the persona of the poet and that of Jeffers occurs in William Stafford's "After Reading Robinson Jeffers." What Stafford senses in Jeffers is not a lonely heroism, but a shared pain that runs so deep it enforces isolation. In Stafford's case, it is the memory of those who "cheated" his father to death and brought about the destruction of his family. Unlike Jeffers, he is not moved to dramatize his pain upon the cosmos, or to seek reconcilement with it as a final source of value. As he moves into a Jeffersian tonality and even rhetoric in the final stanza, his response remains personalized,

his affirmation muted, ironic. Yet if he
rejects a heroic quest for meaning—as
Jeffers himself does in "Meditation on
Saviors" and "Theory of Truth"—his
anger is kindled by that of Jeffers, and his
final imprecation is Jeffers' own:

Dogs are all right, horses,
big still boulders, cathedrals—
there are animals and places I like.
But people, their smell smothers flowers,
their voices clutter and squeak.
This coast will be spoiled for awhile
till cleansed by famine, by fire.

   Hass, Milosz, Williamson, and Stafford
all find Jeffers a formidable if not com-
pletely satisfactory figure. In the poems of
James Tate and William Pitt Root, both
near contemporaries of Williamson, it is
they who are unsatisfactory rather than
Jeffers, or rather the condition they repre-
sent. Tate's poem is indeed called, "Failed
Tribute to the Stonemason of Tor House,
Robinson Jeffers." The mock grandiloqu-
ence of the title suggests the mood of
ironic self-deprecation that informs it.
Tate and his companion arrive in Carmel
to see Tor House in its natural grandeur,
only to find it hedged in by suburban
sprawl. What may have begun as a pil-
grimage or even a high-spirited junket is
quickly reduced to virtual espionage as

*with our cameras cocked we had to
sneak and crawl through trimmed lawns
to even verify the identity of
your strange carbuncular creation,
now rented to trillionaire non-
literary folk from Pasadena.* ★

The very terms in which Jeffers rejected man's self-importance suffer a similar reduction, as if the human present were unworthy to sustain a serious rhetoric at all: "Man *is*/ a puny thing, divorced,/ whether he knows it or not, and/ pays his monthly alimony."[5] Legal relations replace cosmic ones, just as tract housing and concrete replace nature: it is no longer even possible to speak of what has been lost, because language has become too debased to formulate it. Tate himself can hardly state the case, taking refuge in wisecrack and irony, accepting his tourist fate and breaking off in mid-stanza as if, in truth, modern words must fail:

*I seek libation in the Tiki
Bar: naked native ladies are painted
in iridescent orange on velvet cloth:
the whole town loves art.
And I donate this Singapore Sling*

★ A condition happily since rectified, of course, through the purchase of Jeffers' home by the Tor House Foundation.

5. Cf. "The Answer," in *The Selected Poetry of Robinson Jeffers* (New York: Random House, 1959), p. 594.

to the memory of it, and join
the stream of idlers simmering outside.
Much as the hawks circled your head
when you cut stone all afternoon,
kids with funny hats on motorscooters
keep circling the block.
Jeffers, . . .

    William Pitt Root's epistolary poem, "Dear Jeffers," decries the "high priced/ suckertraps" that surround Hawk Tower, which itself had "gone into their hands, their pockets,/ enhanced by your famous hatred." Even protest redounds on the protester; there is profit to be made on prophecy, on moral outrage, and Jeffers' tower is debased in the exact measure of value the labor of his hands and mind put into it. What can survive of a great poet in an age unworthy to receive him? Jeffers himself had devoted much thought to the subject,[6] foreseeing a long decadence, but, Root suggests, even he could not have anticipated the full bitterness and hopelessness of the present. Writing from a Wyoming "still magnificent/ with wilderness," Root can only contemplate the coming disaster without the energy to resist: or perhaps knowing, like Tate, that

---

6. See especially his "Poetry, Gongorism, and a Thousand Years," *The New York Times*, January 18, 1948, sec. 6, p. 18.

outrage in circumstances sufficiently abject seems merely comic. He concludes with bitter irony:

> . . . men hungry for the good life will descend
> innocent of your hawks, gulls, godlike
>   stallions, and women
> with wild eyes will tend them
> as some die, most prosper in the ways men do
>   these days, their families
> dull with generations of decay
> in their hearts, surrounded by the crown jewels
>   of the age—appliances and gadgets
>   designed to make
> life careless. And they work, dear Jeffers. They
>   do work.

Tate and Root use Jeffers to shame an ignoble present. But Jeffers asked not to be judged by his own historical moment or that of his successors, but by what he took to be both the means and the goal of all great art, universality and permanence: "Permanent things are what is needful in a poem, things temporally/ Of great dimension, things continually renewed or always present./ . . . Fashionable and momentary things we need not see nor speak of."[7]

    That standard itself is of course open to judgment, as Tim Hunt suggests in "Thoughts of Jeffers and Tor House." Jef-

---

7. "Point Joe," *Collected Poetry*, I: 90.

fers' very quest for permanence, Hunt asserts, reflects an underlying "horror" of the soft and perishing stuff of which man is made; even in that one element by which he sought to transcend his condition, he was but "an imagination of fire and slime." Yet, however one may measure Jeffers' achievement, the passion of his quest is palpable, and Hunt responds to it with lines that, themselves deeply felt, have finely caught its anguish:

In the photos Tor House seems an outcropping of rock—
the bare headland before Jeffers planted the cypress;
Hawk Tower, just begun, squat and crude as a burial mound.
In one Jeffers stands, grayed like fog
stained wood. In the tall grass, he is a rock washed
by tongues of gray flame that seem to feed
on a man who would burn with a fire beyond ash.

The identification between Jeffers and Tor House runs through many of the poems in this volume, reflecting the sense of his inseparability from the natural world of the coast. In John Brugaletta's, the poet and his house have become one, and the unoccupied attic is likened to the empty shell of the snail, which in turn becomes the void of a God-abandoned universe that rushes toward nothing but its own annihilating collapse:

But that black close of all days,
that great crashing coming-home of the gods,
that striking of the huge tent
that folding of stars inward on themselves and
	endlessly folding—
that closes down everything.
There are no memories of this in the stones,
No tiniest pattern, it seems, will remain for a
	memory.

If even the stones, Jeffers' own symbol of permanence, will retain no trace of our cosmos, then what, Brugaletta asks, addressing both Jeffers and the Old Testament God as "my honest father. . . in the garden," must men do? The only answer is that they must go on, "assuming significance" if for no other reason than that they find in themselves the capacity to do so. The answer is Brugaletta's, but the source, clearly, is Jeffers' own passionate affirmation of meaning in the face of the void.

Jeffers' persona has seemed a particularly masculine one, yet he remains a talismanic figure even for female poets whose concerns would appear, on the surface, to be far removed from his. Diane Wakoski, a political liberal, and Adrienne Rich, a radical feminist, have found in him a necessary pole of resistance, a presence which commands respect and engagement. In Rich's "Yom Kippur 1984," Jeffers is first "the poet" whose evocation of lupine on a California mountain secures the coastal landscape as memorably as Whitman's lilacs does his great elegy,[8] and only then the Robinson Jeffers whose rejection of the multitude she feels impelled to protest. Yet even in insisting on the uniqueness of individuals and affirming her own need for acceptance within the tribe, she confesses to a thirst for separation and solitude as great as her need for solidarity, and finds herself returned again to Jeffers' images, and even his cadences:

*When the winter flood-tides wrench the tower
    from the rock, crumble the prophet's
    headland, and the farms slide into the sea
when leviathan is endangered and Jonah
    becomes revenger
when center and edges are crushed together, the
    extremities crushed together on which the
    world was founded. . .*
                                *what will
    solitude mean?*

Wakoski, too, in "Cap of Darkness," struggles to bridge opposites, to reconcile city and desert, solitude and solidarity, in "a place where paradoxical landscapes/

---

8. See *The Double Axe and Other Poems* (New York: Liveright, 1977), p. 3.

come together." Although there is no direct reference to Jeffers except in the poem's subtitle, "For Robinson Jeffers," he remains an implicit guide in Wakoski's own search for self-definition and her rejection of establishment poetics. In this way too, we are reminded, Jeffers is a continuing presence for those seeking to stake out their own poetic claim, and takes his place in the great dissenting tradition of American letters that descends from Thoreau.

As Milosz reminds us, however, the pull of Jeffers' verse is often greatest at a distance. This is true in the English poet Peter Dale's "Homage to Robinson Jeffers," which takes its point of departure from Jeffers' "The Bed by the Window," and seems to contemplate the wreck of the English coastline no less than California's. For Dale, Jeffers' bedchamber becomes the room of his poetry, admitting only "the odd guest" to its elemental and cleansing force, and giving him at last, as the words of Christ no longer do, a fitting "place to die." Quiet in its intensity and all the more effective for its restraint, Dale's poem, like many of the others in this collection, is a tribute to the sense of awe he evokes as a prophet, teacher, guide, and even more as the poet who, without dogma, has more than any embodied the certainty of religious truth in our time.

In taking him thus, the poets of this generation have paid singular homage to Jeffers' hold on the modern literary imagination, and have begun the longer task of sifting his final importance as well. If, as Jeffers himself believed, the test of great poetry is not the capacity to touch a generation or two but to reach a future millenium, then the verdict will be neither ours to make nor know. Yet of whom else in our time are even some prepared to say, in the bold words of Bill Hotchkiss' "For Robinson Jeffers,"

> *You were the master spirit . . .*
> *Far ages will come to pay you reverence: you saw to*
> *the mystery*
> *And still loved it, you fleshed the bones of the swan.*

THE POET IS DEAD

A Memorial for Robinson Jeffers

WILLIAM EVERSON

*To be read with a full stop
between the strophes, as in a dirge.*

In the evening the dusk
Stipples with lights. The long shore
Gathers darkness in on itself
And goes cold. From the lap of silence
All the tide-crest's pivotal immensity
Lifts into the land.

Snow on the headland,
Rare on the coast of California.
Snow on Point Lobos,
Falling all night,
Filling the creeks and the back country,
The strangely beautiful
Setting of death.

For the poet is dead.
The pen, splintered on the sheer
Excesses of vision, unfingered, falls.
The heart-crookt hand, cold as a stone,
Lets it go down.

The great tongue is dried.
The teeth that bit to the bitterness
Are sheathed in truth.

If you listen
You can hear the field mice
Kick little rifts in the snow-swirls.
You can hear
Time take back its own.

. . .

For the poet is dead.
On the bed by the window,
Where dislike and desire
Killed each other in the crystalline interest,
What remains alone lets go of its light. It
    has found
Finalness. It has touched what it craved:
    the passionate
Darks of deliverance.

At sundown the sea wind,
Burgeoning,
Bled the west empty.

Now the opulent
Treacherous woman called Life
Forsakes her claim. Blond and a harlot
She once drank joy from his narrow loins.
She broke his virtue in her knees.

In the water-gnawn coves of Point Lobos
The white-faced sea otters
Fold their paws on their velvet breasts
And list waveward.

But he healed his pain on the wisdom of
    stone.
He touched roots for his peace.

. . .

For the poet is dead. The gaunt wolf
Crawled out to the edge and died
    snapping.
He said he would. The wolf
Who lost his mate. He said he would carry
    the wound,
The blood-wound of life, to the broken
    edge
And die grinning.

Over the salt marsh the killdeer,
Unrestrainable,
Cry fear against moonset.

And all the hardly suspected
Latencies of disintegration
Inch forward. The skin
Flakes loss. On the death-gripped feet
The toenails glint like eyeteeth
From the pinched flesh.
The caged ribs and the bladed shoulders,
Ancient slopes of containment,
Imperceptibly define the shelves of
    structure,
Faced like rock ridges
Boned out of mountains, absently
    revealed
With the going of the snow.

In the sleeve of darkness the gopher
Tunnels the sod for short grass
And pockets his fill.

. . .

And the great phallus shrinks in the groin,
The seed in the scrotum
Chills.

When the dawn comes in again,
Thoughtlessly,
The sea birds will mew by the window.

For the poet is dead. Beyond the courtyard
The ocean at full tide hunches its bulk.
Groping among the out-thrusts of granite
It moans and whimpers. In the
    phosphorescent
Restlessness it chunks deceptively,
Wagging its torn appendages, dipping and
    rinsing
Its ripped sea rags, its strip-weeded kelp.
The old mother grieves her deathling.
She trundles the dark for her lost child.
She hunts her son.

On the top of the tower
The hawk will not perch tomorrow.

But in the gorged rivermouth
Already the steelhead fight for entry.
They feel fresh water
Sting through the sieves of their salt-
    coarsened gills.
They shudder and thrust.

. . .

So the sea broods. And the aged gull,
Asleep on the water, too stiff to feed,
Spins in a side-rip crossing the surf
And drags down.

This mouth is shut. I say
The mouth is clamped cold.
I tell you this tongue is dried.

But the skull, the skull,
The perfect sculpture of bone!—
Around the forehead the fine hair,
Composed to the severest
Lineaments of thought,
Is moulded on peace.

And the strongly-wrought features,
That keep in the soul's serenest
    achievement
The spirit's virtue,
Set the death mask of all mortality,
The impress of that grace.

In the shoal-champed breakers
One wing of the gull
Tilts like a fin through the ribbon of
    spume
And knifes under.

. . .

And all about there the vastness of night
Affirms its sovereignty. There's not a cliff
Of the coastline, not a reef
Of the waterways, from the sword-thrust
    Aleutians
To the scorpion-tailed stinger Cape
    Horn—
All that staggering declivity
Grasped in the visionary mind and
    established—
But is sunken under the dark ordainment,
Like a sleeper possessed, like a man
Gone under, like a powerful swimmer
Plunged in a womb-death washed out to sea
And worked back ashore.

The gull's eye,
Skinned to the wave, retains the ocean's
Imponderable compression,
And burns yellow.

The poet is dead. I tell you
The nostrils are narrowed. I say again and
    again
The strong tongue is broken.

. . .

But the owl
Quirks in the cypresses, and you hear
What he says. He is calling for something.
He tucks his head for his mate's
Immemorial whisper. In her answering
    voice
He tastes the grace-note of his reprieve.

When fog comes again to the canyons
The redwoods will know what it means.
The giant sisters
Gather it into their merciful arms
And stroke silence.

You smell pine resin laced in the salt
And know the dawn wind has veered.

And on the shelf in the gloom,
Blended together, the tall books emerge,
All of a piece. Transparent as membranes
The thin leaves of paper hug their dark
    thoughts.
They know what he said.

The sea, reaching for life,
Spits up the gull. He falls spread-eagled,
The streaked wings swept on the sand.
Vague fingers of snow, aimlessly deft,
    grope for his eyes.
When the blind head snaps
The beak krakes at the sky.

. . .

Now the night closes.
All the dark's negatory
Decentralization
Quivers toward dawn.

He has gone into death like a stone thrown
    in the sea.

And in far places the morning
Shrills its episodes of triviality and vice
And one man's passing. Could the ears
That hardly listened in life
Care much less now?

Snow on the headland,
The strangely beautiful
Oblique concurrence,
The strangely beautiful
Setting of death.

The great tongue
Dries in the mouth. I told you.
The voiceless throat
Cools silence. And the sea-granite eyes.
Washed in the sibilant waters
The stretched lips kiss peace.

The poet is dead.

Nor will ever again hear the sea lions
Grunt in the kelp at Point Lobos.
Nor look to the south when the grunion
Run the Pacific, and the plunging
Shearwaters, insatiable,
Stun themselves in the sea.

THE STONE-MASON

TIM REYNOLDS

> *The stone-mason seeketh for work in all*
> *manner of hard stone.*
> *When he hath finished it his arms are*
> *destroyed, and he is weary . . . .*

Lying on sand where mountain streams
 break through, I have seen
at night, on bridges, streaks of black
 across the burning stars,
headlights; whose light, passing the
 concrete slats, quite suddenly
shut like a fan: driving the high cliff road,
 coming slowly around
a granite shoulder, I saw once a comber of
 white fog poised
so like a wave, so huge, so heavily, that I
 stopped the car, braced
for the fall: I have watched hawks in
 updraft effortlessly lifting,
wings wide: seen redwoods' strength and
 cypresses' warped endurance;
sea-carved granite headlands plumbing
 sheer down, bicep-curved, to sea;
half-seen deer—seen, but never freshly, all
 this having been claimed by
him who staked out this land, these
 permanences, unalienably for his.
And I have seen him, who quarried out
 and worked this raw existence,
the stone-mason: seen him walking by day
 in shade of the big trees
framing the tower of boulders he hung
 against the sky, back broad

and hard-handed—but bent, but slow,
 after a spent life of building
something more lucid than any visible
 light, lighter than fog,
lifting still higher than hawk-flight, yet
 comprehending most things
hard, pure and durable, something tough
 as backbones of coastal hills
and spacious, like a tower, with a solid
 place to stand on top—
watched him picking his way along rock
 shores at night, alone
under the stars he loves (which, weary
 now, burn steadily, if far,
fragments of an older fury).

Nepenthe, 1958

THE RETURN OF
ROBINSON JEFFERS

ROBERT HASS

I

He shuddered briefly and stared down the
    long valley where the headland rose
And the lean gum trees rattled in the wind
    above Point Sur;
Alive, he had littered the mind's coast
With ghosts of Indians and granite and the
    dead fleshed
Bodies of desire. That work was done
And, whether done well or not, it had
    occupied him
As the hawks and the sea were occupied.
Now he could not say what brought him
    back.
He had imagined resurrection once: the
    lover of a woman
Who lived lonely in a little ranch house up
    the ridge
Came back, dragged from the grave by
    her body's need
To feel under ashen cloud-skies and in the
    astonishments
Of sunrise some truth beyond the daily lie
Of feeding absolute hunger the way a
    young girl might trap meadow lice
To feed a red-tailed hawk she kept
    encaged. She wanted to die once
As the sun dies in pure fire on the farthest
    sea-swells.
She had had enough and more of nights
    when the brain
Flickered and dissolved its little
    constellations and the nerves

Performed their dumb show in the dark
    among the used human smells of
    bedsheets.
So she burned and he came, a ghost in
    khaki and stunned skin,
And she fled with him. He had imagined,
    though he had not written,
The later moment in the pasture, in
    moonlight like pale stone,
When she lay beside him with an after-
    tenderness in all her bones,
Having become entirely what she was,
    though aware that the thing
Beside her was, again, just so much
    cheese-soft flesh
And jellied eye rotting in the pools of
    bone.
Anguish afterwards perhaps, but he had
    not thought afterwards.
Human anguish made him cold.
He told himself the cries of men in war
    were no more conscious
Nor less savage than the shrill repetitions
    of the Steller's jay
Flashing through live oaks up Mal Paso
    Canyon
And that the oaks, rooted and growing
    toward their grace,
Were—as species go—
More beautiful.

2

He had given himself to stone gods.
I imagine him thinking of that woman
While a live cloud of gulls
Plumes the wind behind a trawler
Throbbing toward the last cannery at
  Monterey.
The pelicans are gone which had,
  wheeling,
Written Chinese poems on the sea. The
  grebes are gone
That feasted on the endless hunger of the
  flashing runs
Of salmon. And I imagine that he saw,
  finally,
That though rock stands, it does not
  breed.
He feels specific rage. Feels, obscurely,
  that his sex
Is his, not god-force only, but his own soft
  flesh grown thick
With inconsolable desire. The grebes are
  gone.
He feels a plain man's elegiac tenderness,
An awkward brotherhood with the
  world's numb poor
His poems had despised. Rage and
  tenderness are pain.
He feels pain as rounding at the hips, as
  breasts.
Pain blossoms in his belly like the first
  dark

Stirrings of a child, a surfeit of the love
    that he had bled to rock
And twisted into cypress haunts above the
    cliffs.
He knows he has come back to mourn,
To grieve, womanish, a hundred patient
    years
Along this fragile coast. I imagine the sky's
    arch,
Cloud-swift, lifts him then, all ache in sex
    and breasts,
Beyond the leached ashes of dead fire,
The small jeweled hunger in the seabird's
    eye.

TO ROBINSON JEFFERS

CZESLAW MILOSZ

If you have not read the Slavic poets
so much the better. There's nothing there
for a Scotch-Irish wanderer to seek. They
    lived in a childhood
prolonged from age to age. For them, the
    sun
was a farmer's ruddy face, the moon
    peeped through a cloud and
the Milky Way gladdened them like a
    birch-lined road.
They longed for the Kingdom which is
    always near,
always right at hand. Then, under apple
    trees
angels in homespun linen will come
    parting the boughs and at the
white kolkhoz tablecloth
cordiality and affection will feast (falling
    to the ground at times).

. . .

And you are from surf-rattled skerries.
    From the heaths
where burying a warrior they broke his
    bones
so he could not haunt the living. From the
    sea night
which your forefathers pulled over
    themselves, without a word.
Above your head no face, neither the sun's
    nor the moon's
only the throbbing of galaxies, the
    immutable
violence of new beginnings, of new
    destruction.

All your life listening to the ocean. Black
    dinosaurs
wade where a purple zone of
    phosphorescent weeds
rises and falls on the waves as in a dream.
    And Agamemnon
sails the boiling deep to the steps of the
    palace
to have his blood gush onto marble. Till
    mankind passes
and the pure and stony earth is pounded by
    the ocean.

. . .

Thin-lipped, blue-eyed, without grace or
    hope,
before God the Terrible, body of the
    world.
Prayers are not heard. Basalt and granite.
Above them, a bird of prey. The only
    beauty.

What have I to do with you? From
    footpaths in the orchards,
from an untaught choir and shimmers of a
    monstrance, from flower
beds of rue, hills by the rivers, books
in which a zealous Lithuanian announced
    brotherhood, I come.
Oh, consolations of mortals, futile creeds.

. . .

And yet you did not know what I know.
    The earth teaches
More than does the nakedness of
    elements. No one with impunity
gives to himself the eyes of a god. So
    brave, in a void.
You offered sacrifices to demons: there
    were Wotan and Thor,
the screech of Erinyes in the air, the terror
    of dogs
when Hekate with her retinue of the dead
    draws near.
Better to carve suns and moons on the
    joints of crosses
as was done in my district. To birches and
    firs
give feminine names. To implore
    protection
against the mute and treacherous might
than to proclaim, as you did, an inhuman
    thing.

FOR ROBINSON JEFFERS

ALAN WILLIAMSON

More and more I think about you, and the
    others—
your likes and unlikes—who chose to
    harden their difference
until it was so dense, it would shine of
    itself in the dark;
lived narrow into towers, to the faces of
    wives and children
loved more steadily than most; turned
    their even-planed desks to the ocean;
and built the beds they would die in into
    the stonework
of their hand-made houses, trying to care
    as little
for fame as the dead, or hawks . . .

    Oh, I know
all one might say: that what you fled and
    resented
was the father within; or worse, some
    incapacity
you half-knew in yourself, and could not cure;
that the more your peace was
    accomplished, the harder a spectral
humanity seethed from behind the planted
    forest,
from the cities as you dreamed them . . .
    till the love of yourself you began with
half-recoiled at the self it had made . . .

. . .

And yet . . . to become something simply
because one can imagine it, and it isn't
    there;
to say—as I half-hear you—*the others have
    chosen*
*to elaborate the surface, until it seems to them
    they*
are surface merely—a celluloid barely tingeing
*the blank face of the streets; or else they name
    themselves*
*stones and roots, without eyes. What have they
    left us*
even to wish for? And then, returning: *those*
*who hated me did so not for my faults, but
    because*
*I wished to walk out of myself in a soul and a
    body.*

FAILED TRIBUTE TO THE STONEMASON OF TOR HOUSE

JAMES TATE

We traveled down to see your house,
Tor House, Hawk Tower, in Carmel,
California. It was not quite what
I thought it would be: I wanted it
to be on a hill, with a view of the ocean
unobstructed by other dwellings.
Fifty years ago I know you had
a clean walk to the sea, hopping
from boulder to boulder, the various
seafowl rightly impressed with
your lean, stern face. But today

with our cameras cocked we had to
sneak and crawl through trimmed lawns
to even verify the identity of
your strange carbuncular creation,
now rented to trillionaire non-
literary folk from Pasadena.
Edged in on all sides by trilevel
pasteboard phantasms, it took
a pair of good glasses to barely see
some newlyweds feed popcorn
to an albatross. Man *is*

. . .

a puny thing, divorced,
whether he knows it or not, and
pays his monthly alimony,
his child-support. Year after year
you strolled down to this exceptionally
violent shore and chose your boulder;
the arms grew as the house grew
as the mind grew to exist outside
of time, beyond the dalliance
of your fellows. Today I hate
Carmel: I seek libation in the Tiki

Bar: naked native ladies are painted
in iridescent orange on velvet cloth:
the whole town loves art.
And I donate this Singapore Sling
to the memory of it, and join
the stream of idlers simmering outside.
Much as hawks circled your head
when you cut stone all afternoon,
kids with funny hats on motorscooters
keep circling the block.
Jeffers, . . .

AFTER READING
ROBINSON JEFFERS

WILLIAM STAFFORD

I can't touch anyone.
It was people who cheated my father
and brought his death, worrying
on the road for a living. They killed him.
And my mother, sister, brother—
nobody saved them, strangers
buried them in unmarked ground.

I know the people I meet
didn't wrong me, but they're like those
    others,
dressed like them, their eyes the same.
And their tongues move in their mouths
that way, unreliable,
always explaining something,
too guilt-ridden for words.

Dogs are all right, horses,
big still boulders, cathedrals—
there are animals and places I like.
But people, their smell smothers flowers,
their voices clutter and squeak.
This coast will be spoiled for awhile
till cleansed by famine, by fire.

DEAR JEFFERS

WILLIAM PITT ROOT

A Note from Sheridan to Carmel-by-the-Sea

It's a long way from the queer remote
    silence-making *quawk* of that heron
your words snagged on the wing as I
was being born, Jeffers,
decades ago, in a Minnesota blizzard, and
    you were in a squall of rage
near Big Sur in the place no longer your
    place—
as you foresaw, dragging stone after stone
    to your tower nonetheless
from the live surf and froth of your own
    sweat. Edged in
now by homes No-Man built to live in—
    high priced
suckertraps for those successful in that
    coming world you shunned and
    decried
poem after bitter poem—your stone
    tower, Jeffers, even your stone tower
raised by hand toward the high blue home
of your beloved hawks
toward whom you turned and turned your
    falcon of a face for evidence
of worthiness, is gone into their hands,
    their pockets,
enhanced by your famous hatred, the
    prices rising
with your skydriven fistlike poems
    exactly
abhorring them.

                Where I am, in Wyoming
   still magnificent with wilderness
no sea has breathed on for millions of
      years, the old forces
finding a new grip soon will ream out
ranchers and farmers bewildered by
      profits sudden as true strokes,
      making way
for holes into which men hungry for the
      good life will descend
innocent of your hawks, gulls, godlike
      stallions, and women
with wild eyes will tend them
as some die, most prosper in the ways men
      do these days, their families
dull with generations of decay
in their hearts, surrounded by the crown
      jewels of the age—
appliances and gadgets designed to make
life careless. And they work, dear Jeffers.
   They do work.

THOUGHTS OF JEFFERS
AND TOR HOUSE

TIM HUNT

A man is a soft thing. Soft in mind and
 spirit if not always
the body, though that too turns in its time.
Jeffers had a horror of this, the petty slime,
 and loved therefore
with all the will in him rock
and the hawk's fire eye, the implacable
God of Calvin—a glory he called nature.

Yet like us he would fold with age
and not the edge of rock. Like us
an imagination of fire and slime.
And so the poems and so the house—sea
 granite
rolled from the beach and masoned
into a shell where a hermit crab of a man
might seem to burn with a patient will and
 not the quick
flame of desire or dying.

In the photos Tor House seems an
 outcropping of rock—
the bare headland before Jeffers planted the
 cypress;
Hawk Tower, just begun, squat and crude
 as a burial mound.
In one Jeffers stands, grayed like fog
stained wood. In the tall grass, he is a rock
 washed
by tongues of flame that seem to feed
on a man who would burn with a fire
 beyond ash.

JEFFERS' HOUSE

JOHN BRUGALETTA

1 (Snail)

Here where the land gives up again and
    drifts into sleep under ocean,
in this rock-bordered garden, among the
    wiry rose bushes, the lavender and
    rosemary,
I find you dissolving.
They have spread poison for you like a feast
and you have dined,
thinking perhaps we were cleansing you
    for our table
and you dreamed of entering our
    ferocious mouths,
becoming our snapping hands, our quick
    heads, terrible huge legs.

But you have become slime,
only a shining spot of slime for a little
    while.
Never again will the goddess in you
say to the god,
"Up to the attic with you."
Never again will he go up the narrow,
    narrow stair
past the ceiling of your brown shell.

Now you are shell and are beautiful, a
    beautiful and delicate whorl,
common as a sparrow, unremarkable as a
    word,
perched on the high land, a dry shard of
    bird's egg . . .

2 (Spider)

What is that over her desk?
A pleat of sunlight
and climbing downward a spider, small,
    white.
Before there were men and women,
this spider was.
Before men sat with their families in the
    evening around the fire,
before they could read to their families,
before stone on stone was dealt charms to
    stand,
before introspective apes considered,
before they bargained their ignominious
    bargains with the universe for more
    time,
before they cursed the great Being for
    savaging their lives,
before they gave in and said Yes it is
    horrible but it is beautiful,
this dripping arachnid picked its way up
    the rock cliff face.

3 (Steady State)

And yet you were right:
All the tassels and fringes of verse are
    filthy rags.
But so is everything built of stacked
    words, stacked stones, stacked lives,
    stacked civilizations,
stacked universes waiting to unfurl and
    furl again.

But that black close of all days,
that great crashing coming-home of the
    gods,
that striking of the huge tent,
that folding of stars inward on themselves
    and endlessly folding—
that closing down ends everything.
There are no memories of this in the
    stones.
No tiniest pattern, it seems, will remain
    for a memory.

In the end there is nothing at all,
not even the webbed convergences of
    light.
What begins again will have no past.

. . .

What then would you have us do,
my honest father shining in the garden
    bed?
What except work, embrace, live as well
    as we can,
take death when it comes but never look
    for it,
leave our fragile leavings
never knowing anything for certain
but assuming significance.

On trust, because we can do it,
assuming some significance.

YOM KIPPUR 1984

ADRIENNE RICH

I drew solitude over me, on the long shore.
    ROBINSON JEFFERS, "PRELUDE"

For whoever does not afflict his soul throughout this day, shall be cut off from his people.
    LEVITICUS 23:29

What is a Jew in solitude?
What would it mean not to feel lonely or afraid
far from your own or those you have called your own?
What is a woman in solitude: a queer woman or man?
In the empty street, on the empty beach, in the desert
what in this world as it is can solitude mean?

The glassy, concrete octagon suspended from the cliffs
with its electric gate, its perfected privacy
is not what I mean
the pick-up with a gun parked at a turn-out in Utah or the Golan Heights
is not what I mean
the poet's tower facing the western ocean, acres of forest planted to the east, the woman reading in the cabin, her attack dog suddenly risen
is not what I mean

. . .

Three thousand miles from what I once
    called home
I open a book searching for some lines I
    remember
about flowers, something to bind me to
    this coast as lilacs in the dooryard
    once
bound me back there—yes, lupines on a
    burnt mountainside,
something that bloomed and faded and
    was written down
in the poet's book, forever:
Opening the poet's book
I find the hatred in the poet's heart: . . . *the
    hateful-eyed*
and human-bodied are all about me: you that
    love multitude may have them

. . .

Robinson Jeffers, multitude
is the blur flung by distinct forms against
 these landward valleys
and the farms that run down to the sea; the
 lupines
are multitude, and the torched poppies,
 the grey Pacific unrolling its scrolls of
 surf,
and the separate persons, stooped
over sewing machines in denim dust, bent
 under the shattering skies of harvest
who sleep by shifts in never-empty beds
 have their various dreams
Hands that pick, pack, steam, stitch, strip,
 stuff, shell, scrape, scour, belong to a
 brain like no other
Must I argue the love of the multitude in
 the blur or defend
a solitude of barbed-wire and searchlights,
 the survivalist's final solution, have I a
 choice?

. . .

To wander far from your own or those you
    have called your own
to hear strangeness calling you from far
    away
and walk in that direction, long and far,
    not calculating risk
to go to meet the Stranger without fear or
    weapon, protection nowhere on your
    mind
(the Jew on the icy, rutted road on
    Christmas Eve prays for another Jew
the woman in the ungainly twisting
    shadows of the street: *Make those be a
    woman's footsteps;* as if she could
    believe in a woman's god)

. . .

Find someone like yourself. Find others.
Agree you will never desert each other.
Understand that any rift among you
means power to those who want to do you
    in.
Close to the center, safety; toward the
    edges, danger.
But I have a nightmare to tell: I am trying
    to say
that to be with my people is my dearest
    wish
but that I also love strangers
that I crave separateness
I hear myself stuttering these words
to my worst friends and my best enemies
who watch for my mistakes in grammar
my mistakes in love.
This is the day of atonement; but do my
    people forgive me?
If a cloud knew loneliness and fear, I
    would be that cloud.

. . .

To love the Stranger, to love solitude—am
    I writing merely about privilege
about drifting from the center, drawn to
    edges,
a privilege we can't afford in the world
    that is,
who are hated as being of our kind: faggot
    kicked into the icy river, woman
    dragged from her stalled car
into the mist-struck mountains, used and
    hacked to death
young scholar shot at the university gates
    on a summer evening walk, his prizes
    and studies nothing, nothing availing
    his Blackness
Jew deluded that she's escaped the tribe,
    the laws of her exclusion, the men too
    holy to touch her hand; Jew who has
    turned her back
on *midrash* and *mitzvah* (yet wears the *chai*
    on a thong between her breasts)
    hiking alone
found with a swastika carved in her back at
    the foot of the cliffs (did she die as
    queer or as Jew?)

. . .

Solitude, O taboo, endangered species
on the mist-struck spur of the mountain, I
    want a gun to defend you
In the desert, on the deserted street, I want
    what I can't have:
your elder sister, Justice, her great
    peasant's hand outspread
her eye, half-hooded, sharp and true
And I ask myself, have I thrown courage
    away?
have I traded off something I don't name?
To what extreme will I go to meet the
    extremist?
What will I do to defend my want or
    anyone's want to search for her spirit-
    vision
far from the protection of those she has
    called her own?
Will I find O solitude
your plumes, your breasts, your hair
against my face, as in childhood, your
    voice like the mockingbird's
singing *Yes, you are loved, why else this song?*
in the old places, anywhere?

. . .

What is a Jew in solitude?
What is a woman in solitude, a queer woman or man?
When the winter flood-tides wrench the tower from the rock, crumble the prophet's headland, and the farms slide into the sea
what leviathan is endangered and Jonah become revenger
when center and edges are crushed together, the extremities crushed together on which the world was founded
when our souls crash together, Arab and Jew, howling our loneliness within the tribes
when the refugee child and the exile's child re-open the blasted and forbidden city
when we who refuse to be women and men as women and men are chartered, tell our stories of solitude spent in multitude
in that world as it may be, newborn and haunted, what will solitude mean?

1984–1985

CAP OF DARKNESS

For Robinson Jeffers

DIANE WAKOSKI

He walks on the desert at night,
which is a cool place,
moisture condensing on the succulent
    green bodies
of saguaro and cholla.
Alone, he should be aware of the city street
just a mile away,
and the city beyond that street,
the violence of hot bodies,
but he is

dreaming of a place where paradoxical
    landscapes
come together.

I repudiate the bad voices of my times,
and I repudiate the weak voices whose
    lyrics are better than their judgments.
So, I walk
in the desert
wearing the cap of darkness which I need
    only in the
city, but
like a reverse hero
                    (perhaps, that is
                    what a woman is?
                    a reverse hero?)
I walk naked and unarmed in the city,
putting on the protective cap of darkness
    only when I
am alone,
in the desert.

. . .

How else would I have any honor?
For I am fighting the unknown, the
    invisible, the
ignorance of vision.
I do not need the beautiful silvery invisible
    helmet
to combat the Bostonian anaemic fashion-
mongers who worship fortune on the
    stock market or
the names of old families.
I do not need it to fight fake Zen-masters
    or
arrogant Quakers
or even the key holders to old university
    gates.

No, my battle is with
the ghosts themselves who have
    positioned
the false singers in their ancestral houses
    and given them
position, money and power.

The ghost of greed
is a Rational man, with a good body, a
    sharp brain,
and a very comfortable life.
He offers me a place in one of these old
    brownstones
if I will accept his other converts.

. . .

But I will never convert to ghost life,
even though my battle
out here on the desert
is with ghosts and half-formed beings.
Wearing the cap of invisibility
which covers my silvery moonlike hair
without anything but a book for a weapon
and an orange for temptation

    (birds, birds with gold wings).

He walks in the desert at night,
where silence is an ally.
The city has muggers, rapists, and
    murderers
who edit periodicals, run contests
and serve themselves banquets.
Peace, peace,
I counsel,
no battles are worth the self-destruction,
but on the desert, there is a kind father
    who must be repudiated,
a sad mother who must be buried,
a jealous sister who will steal the silvery
    helmet,
and an inadequate lover
who will, unknowingly, give power
from his false use of moonlight
and his ignorance of the sun;

. . .

alone, alone,
not peace, but the battle with fashion
conducted in a place where glittering cities
    rise and
fall, with the breath of a sleeping person.

Who is that person?
The sleeping one
whose breath patterns so much?

The man who walks on the desert at night,
so close to the city,
not knowing the city itself,
but himself becoming the blazing lights,
the dark buildings with scattered
    illuminated windows,
and I, standing there,
invisible,
even though the helmet of night now
    belongs to a thief,
knowing the truth,
seeing the city and the desert as one
finally accepting the sand as my carpet,
the light as my hair,
the snakes as companions,
living in a city of cactus
which holds all the moisture needed
                        for existence.

HOMAGE TO ROBINSON JEFFERS

PETER DALE

You chose the bed by the sea window
        for a good deathbed
when you built the house. You had it
        waiting,
letting only the odd guest sleep there,
not knowing its purpose,
yourself perhaps amused, as Death with
        you.

I don't know whether you did die
        in that bed by the sea window.
I hope you did. It is a small right,
like a birthright, the death-right
that we have betrayed like so much else
in this canned world that clutters the sea-
        rocks.

Your room that I have never seen
        I have always imagined,
rock-clean, relentless as your rhythm,
clear with dawnlight or the storm light,
noise of the great sea crashing beyond.
How I envy that clarity.

Wherever I reach my end, Jeffers,
        it will be in that sea room.
You whose words live on
have given me, unlike the Christ,
a place to die.

FOR ROBINSON JEFFERS

WILLIAM HOTCHKISS

I

You were the master spirit: you saw
>through to the terrible agony.
Of God's self-immolation, the world-
>hawk that devours its own entrails
To give birth to itself in serene beauty.

You were the father: do your ashes sleep in
>the peace they desired?
The great waves still chew at the coast
>rocks, but human tenure is brief.
In the awful power of your lines, you
>pointed the way.

II

I stare east toward the high, white peaks of
>the Sierra;
The tall wild plum is in full bloom, white,
>and white moths
Dance among the yellow mustard flowers.
>The sky
Is immense and blue, it leaps eastward
>from these greening foothills
And disappears beyond the far white rim.
>But here the wind
Flows on a soft steadiness from the south,
>bringing warmth.

III

The dance of generation is patient and
	certain; it continues
All but imperceptible, fecund and
	lecherous. It knows the earth
Must be aroused, knows it is fearful. This
	wind will stroke the green thighs
And touch its tongue to the swelling buds,
	will not be satisfied
Until they all have flowered.

IV

Yet now on the easy wind, two redtailed
	hawks have found a buoyant current
They lie upon it, together, then apart, and
	once more together.
The sunlight burns their feathers into
	shining.

V

I close my eyes to see a rain squall over the
	ocean, the vast glare of the sun
Sheening the blue-gray immensity of
	ocean westward from Pico Blanco, I
	hear the cries
Of the birds of the coast, shadows and
	brightness. I smell the good salt air.

VI

This mild spring day, quite drunk with
    blossoming, obscures the long vision:
And yet there are storms to come, huge
    storms of human passion
And nerve-burning fire. The death-dance
    continues, the earth shifts slightly,
And the molten rock spews forth in red
    rivers; our promised land is before us
But the earth wrenches open, the granite
    splits.

VII

You have peace. The daemon behind the
    screen of sea and rock
Has called you down—so now that angry
    spirit rich with patience
Threads earth where the big creek tumbles
    through orange-gray cliffs
To slip across the sand and join the sea: and
    now we seem to hear the hard old
    voice
In loving curses through the ever-restless
    waves.

VIII

Far ages to come will pay you reverence:
    you saw to the mystery
And still loved it, you fleshed the bones of
    the swan.

POET, BE WITH ME

for Robinson Jeffers

ROBERT ZALLER

Bound for darkness, the suburban sky
takes a last emblem: a spine-shaft
of cloud feathered by vertebrae
lung-light yet firm as crystal
the sun a red burl below
adrift like a wandering searchlight.
I wade into traffic to watch it
till the image grows vague, the bonds
    dissolve,
and darker dusk raises up A & S
First Federal and the Miracle Mile
into their daily instant of ruin.

Poet, be with me: this is your kind of sky,
might even be you if that theory holds,
Deus sive natura.
I walk here and get my living
and slowly the ache of flight swells
the useless arms, forgotten wings
and calling on you, calling on strength
I try to stay where I am
and do what I must do
as if I had never dreamed a great hawk
had skimmed me or the sky
was the open breast of a god.

ACKNOWLEDGMENTS

"The Poet is Dead." Copyright ©1978 by William Everson. Reprinted from *The Veritable Years* with the permission of Black Sparrow Press, 24 Tenth Street, Santa Rosa, CA.

"The Stone-Mason." Copyright ©1964 by Tim Reynolds. Reprinted from *Ryoanji and Other Poems* with the permission of Harcourt Brace Jovanovich, Publishers.

"The Return of Robinson Jeffers." Copyright ©1973 by Robert Hass. Reprinted from *Field Guide* by permission of Yale University Press.

"To Robinson Jeffers." Copyright ©1973 by Czeslaw Milosz. Reprinted from *Selected Poems* by Czeslaw Mislosz, first published by The Ecco Press in 1980.

"For Robinson Jeffers." Copyright ©1973 by Alan Williamson. Reprinted from *Presences* by permission of Alfred A. Knopf, Inc.

"Failed Tribute to the Stonemason of Tor House." Reprinted from *The Oblivion Ha-Ha* (Atlantic, Little, Brown, 1970), by permission of James Tate.

"After Reading Robinson Jeffers." Copyright © by William Stafford.

"Dear Jeffers." Copyright ©1981 by William Pitt Root. Reprinted from *Rea-*

sons for Going It on Foot by permission of Atheneum Publishers, Inc.

"Thoughts of Jeffers and Tor House." Copyright © by Tim Hunt. This poem appeared earlier in *Lake Country Diamond*, published by INTERTEXT of Anchorage, Alaska, and is reprinted by permission.

"Jeffers' House." Copyright © by John Brugaletta.

"Yom Kippur 1984." Copyright ©1986 by Adrienne Rich. Reprinted from *Your Native Land, Your Life: Poems by Adrienne Rich*, by permission of the author and the publisher, W. W. Norton & Company, Inc.

"Cap of Darkness." Copyright ©1980 by Diane Wakoski. Reprinted from the book of the same title with the permission of Black Sparrow Press, 24 Tenth Street, Santa Rosa, CA.

"Homage to Robinson Jeffers." Copyright © by Peter Dale.

"For Robinson Jeffers." Copyright ©1978 by Bill Hotchkiss. Reprinted from *Climb to the High Country: Poems by Bill Hotchkiss*, by permission of W. W. Norton & Company, Inc.

"Poet, Be With Me." Copyright ©1985 by Robert Zaller. This poem first appeared in *The Cedarmere Review* (Autumn, 1985).

*Designed and typeset
by Wilsted & Taylor
in Mergenthaler Bembo
Printed by Malloy Lithographing, Inc.*